Ontario

VT INCEPIT   SIC PERMANET

FIDELIS

Ontario

Rennay Craats

WEIGL EDUCATIONAL PUBLISHERS

Published by Weigl Educational Publishers Limited
6325 10 Street SE
Calgary, Alberta, Canada
T2H 2Z9
Web site: www.weigl.com

We acknowledge the financial support of the Government of Canada through the Book Publishing
Industry Development Program (BPIDP) for our publishing activities.

National Library of Canada Cataloguing in Publication Data
Craats, Rennay, 1973-
  Ontario / Rennay Craats.
  (Canadian sites and symbols)
  Includes index.
  ISBN 1-55388-026-9
  1. Provincial emblems--Ontario--Juvenile literature.
2. Heraldry--Ontario--Juvenile literature. I. Title. II. Series.
CR213.05C72 2003   j929.6'09713   C2003-910532-6

Printed in the United States of America
1 2 3 4 5 6 7 8 9 0   07 06 05 04 03

Project Coordinator: Donald Wells
Design: Janine Vangool
Layout: Virginia Boulay
Copy Editor: Tina Schwartzenberger
Photo Researcher: Ellen Bryan

Photograph Credits
Every reasonable effort has been made to trace ownership and to obtain permission to reprint
copyright material. The publishers would be pleased to have any errors or omissions brought to
their attention so that they may be corrected in subsequent printings.

Cover: Horseshoe Falls (**MaXx Images**); **Archives of Ontario, Government of Ontario Art Collection:**
page 6 (619857); **Barrett & MacKay:** pages 4, 11B, 14, 21T, 22; **Canadian Tourism Commission:** pages 3B,
20; **Corel Corporation:** pages 3M, 9, 12, 13B, 15, 16, 17T, 23; **Geovisuals:**
page 17B; **Government of Ontario™:** pages 1, 8; **Lampo Communications Inc.:** pages 3T, 5, 7;
Courtesy of Laurentian University: page 11T; **Legislative Assembly of Ontario:** page 19; **Ontario
Legislative Assembly Interparliamentary and Public Relations Branch:** page 18; **Courtesy of
the Ontario Tourism Marketing Partnership:** page 10; **Parks Canada Photo/Brian Morin:** page
21B; **Tom Stack and Associates:** page 13T (**J. Gerlach**).

Contents

Introduction

Canada is a large country. The ten Canadian provinces
and three territories cover a vast amount of land.
From one province or territory to another,
the people, lifestyles, land, and animals are
quite different. Each province and territory
has its own **identity**. The provinces
and territories use **symbols**
to represent this
identity. This
book looks
at the symbols
that represent
the province
of Ontario.

Yukon
Territory

Nunavut

Northwest
Territories

British
Columbia

Manitoba

Alberta

Saskatchewan

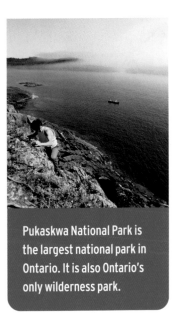

Pukaskwa National Park is
the largest national park in
Ontario. It is also Ontario's
only wilderness park.

Ontario is a large province in central Canada. Ontario borders Manitoba on the west and Quebec on the east. It also borders four of the Great Lakes—Erie, Huron, Ontario, and Superior. The Saint Lawrence River is east of the province. People often think of bustling cities when they think about Ontario. The province also has forests and lakes. The symbols of Ontario stand for the province's natural beauty and its economic strength.

Toronto is the capital city of Ontario. It is also Canada's largest city.

Canada's national capital, Ottawa, is in Ontario.

Ontario covers 1,068,580 square kilometres (412,581 square miles).

Ontario is home to about one-third of Canada's population. Most of these people live in southern Ontario.

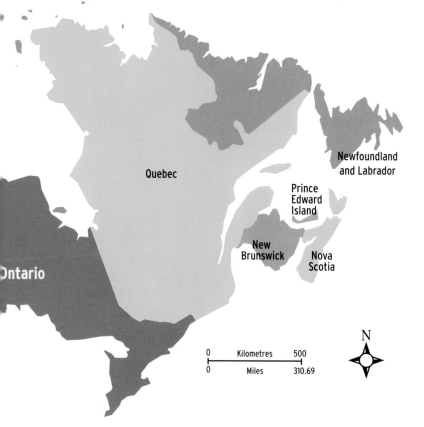

Quebec

Newfoundland and Labrador

Prince Edward Island

New Brunswick

Nova Scotia

Ontario

0   Kilometres   500
0   Miles   310.69

N

What's in a Name?

Before Canada was a country, the area that is now Ontario had different names. It was called Upper Canada in 1791. Most of the people who lived in Upper Canada spoke English. Upper Canada based its laws and government on Great Britain's laws and government. In the mid-1800s, Ontario and Quebec joined to become the United Province of Canada. In this union, Ontario was often referred to as Canada West. When Canada became a country in 1867, Ontario became an independent province.

When Ontario became a province in 1867, the Legislature of Ontario met in the old Parliament Buildings on King Street in Toronto.

Ontario's name came from the shimmering bodies of water in the province. The word *Ontario* comes from the Iroquois word that means "beautiful lake" or "shining water." Water covers about one-sixth of Ontario. The province has 250,000 lakes. Unlike many other provinces, Ontario does not have an official nickname. This does not mean it is not called by other names. It is often referred to as the Heartland Province. This is because it is found near the centre of the country.

Ontario's many waterways provide people with a place to have fun and relax as well as a means of transportation. About 158,654 square kilometres (61,257 square miles) of Ontario is fresh water.

Fun Facts

Ontario's license plates describe the province as "Yours to Discover."

More than half of Ontario's population has British ancestors. The province has many historical sites that celebrate Great Britain's settlement and protection of Ontario.

The population of Ontario was about 11.5 million in 2000. By 2028, Ontario's population is expected to reach more than 15 million.

In 1844, the first suspension bridge in Canada opened in Ottawa, Ontario.

Coat of Arms Closeup

Canadian provinces and territories all have their own coat of arms. A coat of arms is a special design that represents a group or region. Ontario's coat of arms was created in 1868. The animals on either side of the shield and the crest above the shield were both added in 1909 to create the coat of arms. Ontario's coat of arms has been **stylized** since it was created.

VT INCEPIT

SIC PERMANET

FIDELIS

Fun Facts

Ontario's official colours are green and gold. These colours appear on the coat of arms.

The Cross of St. George honours King George III, who ruled the colony when the shield was created.

Features

The crest is a black bear standing on a green and gold wreath. The crest sits above the shield.

Moose

A moose stands on one side of the shield. A deer stands on the other side. These animals were some of the original residents of Ontario.

The top of the shield shows the Cross of St. George. This celebrates the British **heritage** of many people in Ontario.

Three golden maple leaves on a green background are on the bottom part of the shield. The leaves represent the common maple trees found in the province.

A banner flows beneath the shield and supporters. It displays the province's motto *Ut incepit Fidelis sic permanet*, Latin for "Loyal She Began, Loyal She Remains."

Flying the Flag

In 1965, the Ontario government passed the Flag Act. This law describes the design of the official provincial flag. The province's flag has a solid red background. The Union Jack is in the flag's top left corner. This is the flag of Great Britain. The Union Jack represents the close relationship Ontario has with Great Britain. In the bottom right corner of Ontario's flag is the provincial shield. This is the same shield found on the official coat of arms.

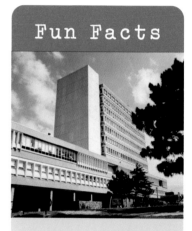

The Franco-Ontarian flag was displayed for the first time in 1975 outside Laurentian University in Sudbury. The flag became official in 2001.

In 2001, a government act—the Franco-Ontarian Flag Act—created another official flag for Ontario. This flag became an official symbol of Ontario's large French-speaking community. The Franco-Ontarian flag is divided in half down the centre. On one side is a white lily on a green background. The other side displays a green trillium on a white background. The trillium is Ontario's official flower. The lily is a symbol of French culture. The colours green and white represent summer and winter in Ontario.

Lake Superior is the largest of the Great Lakes. It could contain all the other Great Lakes plus three more lakes the size of Lake Erie. Waves on Lake Superior have been known to reach more than 6 metres (20 feet) high.

Loonie Birds

Ontario is home to many animals. Polar bears roam along the shores of Hudson Bay in the north. Skunks, squirrels, and porcupines live throughout the province. These animals are often found in city communities. Ontario's forests are home to black bears, foxes, wildcats, and wolves. Caribou, deer, and moose are commonly seen in northern Ontario. Bass, pickerel, pike, and trout can be found in the province's many lakes and rivers. The Great Lakes are home to animals such as eels, herring, and whitefish.

There are more than 75,000 black bears in Ontario. Black bears hibernate in the winter.

Fun Facts

Birds such as crows, pigeons, robins, seagulls, and sparrows are common sights in Ontario's cities. Finches, hawks, jays, starlings, and woodpeckers can be found in country, or rural, areas. Ontario's freshwater lakes and rivers are home to the province's official bird, the common loon. The common loon became the official provincial bird in 1994. The loon was chosen over the American robin, Canada goose, mallard, ruby-throated hummingbird, and great blue heron. The loon appears on the Canadian $1 coin, nicknamed the "loonie."

Although many types of snakes live in Ontario, only the Massasauga rattler is poisonous.

Ontario is home to the five-lined skink. It is the only lizard in eastern Canada.

Small animals, including groundhogs, mink, muskrats, otters, and rabbits, make their homes in Ontario.

Loons are known for their distinct sounds. They make a laughing noise, and they have a wolf-like cry.

Eastern White Pine Trees and White Trilliums

Ontario is covered by forests. Beech, elm, maple, and oak trees are common in southern Ontario. In the north, balsam fir, black spruce, and jack pine trees grow. Fir, pine, spruce, tamarack, and walnut trees live in central Ontario. Wildflowers and plants are scattered throughout these areas. Daisies, irises, lilies, milkweed, Queen Anne's lace, roses, and yarrows brighten the forest floors and wilderness areas. Ontario even has berry bushes, including blackberry, blueberry, cranberry, gooseberry, and raspberry.

Trilliums are called "wake robins." Trilliums bloom in early spring when robins begin to return to Ontario after the winter.

It was difficult for Ontario to choose an official flower and tree because so many different kinds of plants and trees grow in the province. The eastern white pine was named Ontario's official tree in 1984. This tree has been important since pioneers first settled in Ontario. Early settlers sold the tree to shipbuilders. The white trillium, Ontario's official flower since 1937, blooms throughout the province. The image of a trillium is found on the official logo of the provincial government. It also appears on the Franco-Ontarion flag.

Some people thought Ontario's official flower should be the dandelion, orange lily, or posy.

Ontario's forests also contain ash, hickory, poplar, and red cedar trees. Chestnut, magnolia, and sassafras trees grow in the southern parts of the province.

The northernmost part of Ontario is **tundra**. Trees cannot grow in this area. Only lichens, mosses, and small shrubs can live in this harsh **environment**.

Eastern white pines can live to be 450 years old. They are often planted in areas that have been logged because they grow very quickly.

Emblems of the Earth

Mineral emblems show the importance of minerals to a province's **economy**. The amethyst was chosen as Ontario's mineral symbol in 1975. Amethyst is a purple stone in a crystal form. It is found in Bancroft, North Bay, and Thunder Bay. The amethyst is rarely found in other parts of Canada. This made the amethyst a perfect choice for the province's mineral. The amethyst is often set in rings and made into necklace pendants. In ancient times, wearing amethyst was believed to cause lovely dreams.

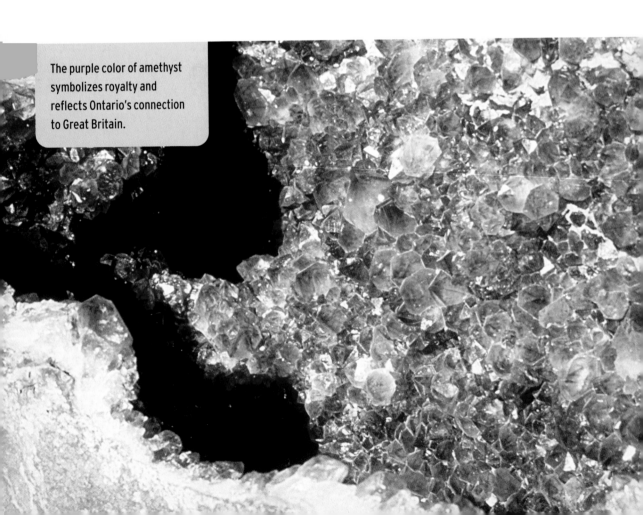

The purple color of amethyst symbolizes royalty and reflects Ontario's connection to Great Britain.

Fun Facts

Ontario has many other valuable minerals. Gold has been mined throughout the province since the early 1900s. Ontario's gold fields provide more than 40 percent of Canada's gold. Uranium is another mineral that is mined in Ontario. Uranium is found in Bancroft, Blind River, and Elliot Lake. Ontario is also Canada's leading producer of cobalt and magnesium. These resources are found along the **Canadian Shield**. Minerals found in southern Ontario include clay, gravel, salt, and sand. These construction materials are important to the province's economy.

Natural gas and petroleum are found south of Lake Huron.

The first oil field in North America was developed in Oil Springs, near Sarnia, Ontario.

The water of Niagara Falls has been used as an energy source since the 1750s. It has been producing electricity since 1905.

The mining industry contributed $5.7 billion to Ontario's economy in 2002.

The Hemlo gold mine began operating in 1985. It is estimated that the mine will produce 623,690 kilograms (22 million ounces) of gold by the time it finishes production.

A Symbolic Staff

Many provinces have an official mace. A mace is an ornamental stick that is carried as a symbol of authority. It represents the power of the government. Ontario has had a few different maces. Some were very fancy. Others were plain. Ontario's current mace was created after **Confederation** in 1867. It is based on Canada's national mace.

There are 103 seats in Ontario's parliament. Elected members are called Members of Provincial Parliament (MPP). Ontario is the only province that uses this title. The Legislative Assembly is also known as Queen's Park.

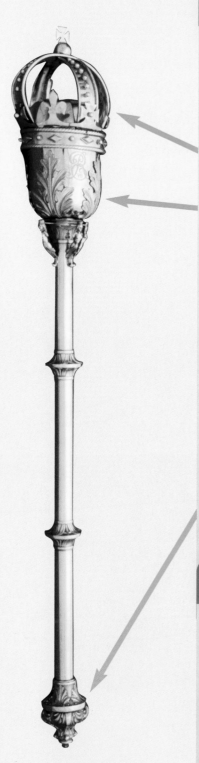

Features

The mace is made of copper and covered in gold.

A crown sits on top of the mace. It honours the British **monarchy**.

The cup is about 20 centimetres (8 inches) long.

When King Edward VII became the ruler of Great Britain, the mace was changed. The letters "V.R." for Victoria Regina had been engraved in the mace's cup. In 1902, these initials were replaced with "E.R." for Edwardus Rex to honour the new monarch.

The club end of the mace looks like a flattened ball. It is rounded at the bottom and flat at the top. It has a design of raised leaves at the end of the club.

Fun Facts

American soldiers stole Ontario's wooden mace in 1813. They took it during an attack on York, the early name for the city of Toronto. The mace was returned in 1934 to celebrate Toronto's 100th anniversary.

Ontario bought its current mace in 1867 for $200.

Special Places

Each territory and province has special places that it protects and celebrates. These places often represent the province's heritage and identity. Ontario's special places include more than 250 provincial parks. The largest provincial park is Algonquin Park. It is located about 250 kilometres (155 miles) north of Toronto. The province also boasts six national parks. Point Pelee National Park has 20 kilometres (12.4 miles) of beautiful sandy beaches on Lake Erie. Georgian Bay Islands National Park is known for its strange rock formations. Millions of people visit these parks each year. The government protects these natural areas to make sure the environment can be enjoyed by visitors for many years.

Algonquin Provincial Park has 7,725 square kilometres (2,982 square miles) of forests, lakes, and rivers. This type of wilderness once covered all of Ontario.

It is not only natural areas that are special to the people of Ontario. There are also many historical sites in Ontario. For example, Woodside at Kitchener was the home of former Prime Minister William Lyon Mackenzie King. Fort Saint Joseph is another special site. This fur trade centre was established on an island between Lake Superior and Lake Huron. Military sites, including a defense post from the late 1700s at Amherstburg and a British fort from the War of 1812, are protected historic parks in Ontario.

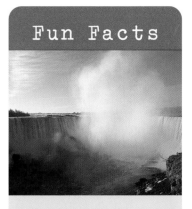

Fun Facts

Niagara Falls is a popular place to visit. The Canadian side of this attraction is called Horseshoe Falls. The water on Horseshoe Falls drops about 53 metres (174 feet). The American side of the falls is located in New York state.

Other national parks in Ontario are Bruce Peninsula National Park, Fathom Five National Marine Park, Pukaskwa National Park, and Saint Lawrence Islands National Park.

Fort George was the headquarters of the British Army in southern Ontario during the War of 1812.

Quiz

Based on what you have read, see if you can answer the following questions:

1.   What is the capital city of Ontario?

2.   Where does the word *Ontario* come from?

3.   Which two animals are on either side of the coat of arms?

4.   What appears in the top left corner of the provincial flag?

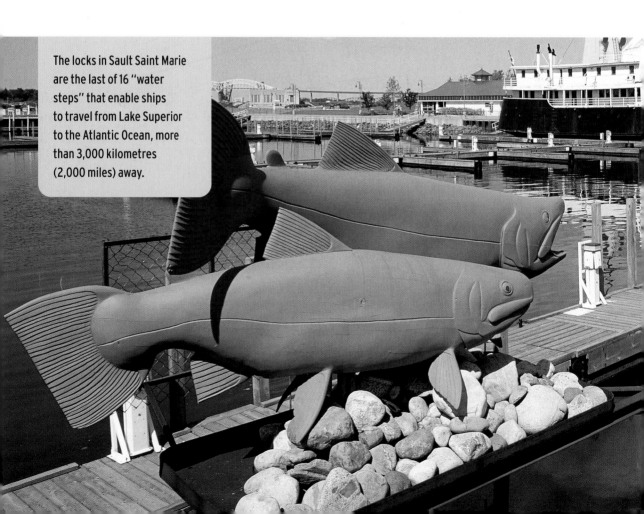

The locks in Sault Saint Marie are the last of 16 "water steps" that enable ships to travel from Lake Superior to the Atlantic Ocean, more than 3,000 kilometres (2,000 miles) away.

5.   What is the official bird of Ontario?

6.   Name the official mineral of Ontario.

7.   How many national parks are located in Ontario?

8.   What is the provincial flower of Ontario?

8. The white trillium

7. Six

6. The amethyst

5. The common loon

4. The British flag, the Union Jack

3. A moose and a deer

2. The Iroquois word for "beautiful lake" or "shining water"

1. Toronto

Ottawa, Ontario, hosts the Canadian Tulip Festival every spring. For 19 days, visitors can see more than 300,000 tulips in full bloom. The Tulip Festival also offers concerts and parades.

Glossary

Canadian Shield: an area of ancient rock that covers part of Canada

Confederation: the joining of the Canadian provinces to form one country

economy: the system of trade and industry that creates the wealth of a community

environment: the area in which something exists or lives

heritage: something handed down from earlier generations

identity: the qualities that make one person or thing different from all others

monarchy: a nation or state ruled by a king or queen

stylized: a style in which there are only a few simple details

symbols: things that stand for something else

tundra: a large, treeless plain in the Arctic

Index